Classical Sheet Music For Alto Saxophone With Alto Saxophone & Piano Duets Book 2

Michael Shaw

Copyright © 2015 Michael Shaw. All rights reserved. Including the right to reproduce this book or portions thereof, in any form. No part of this text may be reproduced in any form without the express written permission of the author.

Music Arrangements. All music arrangements in this book by **Michael Shaw** Copyright © 2015

ISBN: 1517675693
ISBN-13: 978-1517675691

www.mikesmusicroom.co.uk

Contents

Introduction	
Fur Elise: Alto Saxophone	1
Fur Elise: Alto Saxophone & Piano	2
Theme From Jupiter: Alto Saxophone	4
Theme From Jupiter: Alto Saxophone & Piano	6
Radetzky March: Alto Saxophone	9
Radetzky March: Alto Saxophone & Piano	10
La Donna E Mobile (From Rigoletto): Alto Saxophone	12
La Donna E Mobile (From Rigoletto): Alto Saxophone & Piano	14
Valse Lente: Alto Saxophone	17
Valse Lente: Alto Saxophone & Piano	18
Eine Kleine Nachtmusik: Alto Saxophone	21
Eine Kleine Nachtmusik: Alto Saxophone & Piano	22
Etude: Alto Saxophone	24
Etude: Alto Saxophone & Piano	26
Liebestraum: Alto Saxophone	30
Liebestraum: Alto Saxophone & Piano	32
Wedding March (Here Comes The Bride): Alto Saxophone	36
Wedding March (Here Comes The Bride): Alto Saxophone & Piano	38
Sonata In C Major: Alto Saxophone	42
Sonata In C Major: Alto Saxophone & Piano	44
About The Author	48

Introduction

The sheet music in this book has been arranged for Alto Saxophone. There are two versions of every piece in this book. The first version is an Alto Saxophone only arrangement, the second version is an Alto Saxophone and piano accompaniment arrangement. Skill level for this book is a little more advanced than book 1 and varies from Grade 2 to Grade 4 depending on which piece you are playing. The piano parts in this book can be played on a piano, keyboard or organ.

As well as playing duets with piano in this book you can also play together in a duet or ensemble with other instruments with a classical sheet music book for that instrument. All arrangements are the same and keys are adjusted for B flat, E flat, F and C instruments so everything sounds correct. Piano parts for all instrument books are in the same key.

To get a book for your instrument choose from the *Classical Sheet Music Book 2 with Piano Duets* series. Instruments in this series include, Clarinet, Tenor Saxophone, Alto Saxophone, Oboe, Trumpet, French Horn and Trombone.

Check out my author page to view these books.

Author Page US
 amazon.com/Michael-Shaw/e/B00FNVFJGQ/

Author Page UK
 amazon.co.uk/Michael-Shaw/e/B00FNVFJGQ/

Fur Elise
Alto Sax

Beethoven

Fur Elise
Alto Sax & Piano

Beethoven

Theme From Jupiter
Alto Sax
Gustav Holst

Theme From Jupiter
Alto Sax & Piano

Gustav Holst

Radetzky March
Alto Sax
Johann Strauss

Radetzky March

Alto Sax & Piano

Johann Strauss

La Donna E Mobile
Alto Sax

Giuseppe Verdi

La Donna E Mobile

Alto Sax & Piano

Giuseppe Verdi

Valse Lente
Alto Sax

Leo Delibes

Valse Lente
Alto Sax & Piano

Leo Delibes

19

Eine Kleine Nachtmusik
Alto Sax
Mozart

Eine Kleine Nachtmusik
Alto Sax & Piano

Mozart

Etude
Alto Sax

Chopin

Etude
Alto Sax & Piano

Chopin

Liebestraum
Alto Sax

Franz Liszt

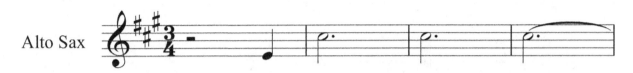

Liebestraum
Alto Sax & Piano

Franz Liszt

33

Wedding March
Alto Sax

Richard Wagner

Wedding March
Alto Sax & Piano

Richard Wagner

39

Sonata In C Major
Alto Sax
Mozart

Sonata In C Major
Alto Sax & Piano

Mozart

About the Author

Mike works as a professional musician and keyboard music teacher. Mike has been teaching piano, electronic keyboard and electric organ for over thirty years and as a keyboard player worked in many night clubs and entertainment venues.

Mike has also branched out in to composing music and has written and recorded many new royalty free tracks which are used worldwide in TV, film and internet media applications. Mike is also proud of the fact that many of his students have gone on to be musicians, composers and teachers in their own right.

You can connect with Mike at:

Facebook
facebook.com/keyboardsheetmusic

Soundcloud
soundcloud.com/audiomichaeld

YouTube
youtube.com/user/pianolessonsguru

I hope this book has helped you with your music, if you have received value from it in any way, then I'd like to ask you for a favour: would you be kind enough to leave a review for this book on Amazon? It'd be greatly appreciated!

Thank You
Michael Shaw

Made in the USA
Monee, IL
12 May 2021